The Home Front in the South

Diane Smolinski

Series Consultant:
Lieutenant Colonel G.A. LoFaro

Heinemann Library
Chicago, Illinois

© 2001 Reed Educational & Professional Publishing
Published by Heinemann Library,
an imprint of Reed Educational & Professional Publishing,
Chicago, IL
Customer Service 888-454-2279
Visit our website at www.heinemannlibrary.com

Designed by Herman Adler Design
Printed in Hong Kong

05 04 03 02 01
10 9 8 7 6 5 4 3 2 1

Library of Congress Cataloging-in-Publication Data
Smolinski, Diane, 1950-
    The home front in the South / Diane Smolinski.
    p. cm. -- (Americans at war. Civil War)
    Includes bibliographical references and index.
    ISBN 1-58810-100-2
    1. United States--History--Civil War, 1861-1865--Social
aspects--Juvenile literature. 2. Confederate States of
America--Social conditions--Juvenile literature. I. Title.
E468.9 .S665 2001
973.7'1--dc21

                                        00-012486

Acknowledgments
The author and publishers are grateful to the following for
permission to reproduce copyright material: p. 3 Georgia
Department of Archives and History; p. 5 Collection of
Marie and Boleslaw Mastai; p. 6–7, 15, 18, 23 bottom
Library of Congress; p. 7, 8, 9, 12–13, 16, 19 right, 21, 22,
24, 25, 26, 28–27, 29 Corbis; p. 10 University of North
Carolina; p. 11 Museum of the Confederacy; p. 15 inset
Archive Photos; p. 17 Richard T. Norwitz/Corbis; p. 18 inset
Georgia Department of Archives and History; p. 19 left
Underwood & Underwood/Corbis; p. 20 Medford Historical
Society/Corbis; p. 23 top Ewing Galloway/Index Stock
Imagery/PictureQuest; p. 27 National Archives.

Cover photograph Courtesy of The Museum of the
Confederacy, Richmond, Virginia.

About the Author
Diane Smolinski is a teacher for the Seminole County School
District in Florida. She earned B.S. of Education degrees
from Duquesne University and Slippery Rock University in
Pennsylvania. For the past fourteen years, Diane has taught
the Civil War curriculum to fourth and fifth graders. She was
also instrumental in writing the pioneer room curriculum,
indicative of the Civil War era, for the school district's
student history museum. Diane lives with her husband,
two daughters, and a cat.

About the Consultant
G.A. LoFaro is a lieutenant colonel in the U.S. Army currently
stationed at Fort McPherson, Georgia. After graduating from
West Point, he was commissioned in the infantry. He has
served in a variety of positions in the 82nd Airborne
Division, the Ranger Training Brigade, and Second Infantry
Division in Korea. He has a Masters Degree in U.S. history
from the University of Michigan and is completing his Ph.D
in U.S. History at the State University of New York at Stony
Brook. He has also served six years on the West Point faculty
where he taught military history to cadets.

Some words are shown in bold, **like this.**
You can find out what they mean by looking in the glossary.

Contents

The Confederacy Is Formed

Citizens throughout the United States of America had been arguing about slavery and states' rights for many years. In 1860, no more compromises could be reached.

Northern States

Leaders in the northern states wanted to stop slavery from spreading. They thought that newly admitted states or **territories** should not allow slavery. Many people throughout the North, including the leaders in the **federal** government, strongly held the opinion that no state had the right to separate from the **Union.**

Southern States

Most citizens and leaders in the southern states believed that each state or territory should be allowed to decide individually whether to allow slavery. Political leaders in South Carolina did not see any solution to this ongoing disagreement. They decided that South Carolina should **secede** from the United States of America, or Union, in December of 1860. Soon, six more southern states seceded as well.

Many southerners were upset by the election of Abraham Lincoln as president of the United States. They feared he might call for an end to slavery. On February 4, 1861, in Montgomery, Alabama, seven southern states announced that they were now a new nation.

The Confederate States of America

South Carolina
December 20, 1860

Mississippi
January 9, 1861

Florida
January 10, 1861

Alabama
January 11, 1861

Georgia
January 19, 1861

Louisiana
January 26, 1861

Texas
February 23, 1861

After Union soldiers surrendered Fort Sumter to Confederate troops, four more southern states seceded.

Virginia
April 17, 1861

Tennessee
May 7, 1861

Arkansas
May 6, 1861

North Carolina
May 20, 1861

These dates are the days the states voted in conventions on the ordinances of secession.

This Confederate battle flag was designed in Savannah, Georgia, in May 1961. Many different battle flags were flown during the Civil War.

Jefferson Davis (1808–1889)

Jefferson Davis was elected president of the Confederate States of America on February 18, 1861. Just 53 days later, he gave the order to fire upon Fort Sumter, beginning the Civil War. Davis supported states' rights, including the right to own slaves. He firmly believed southerners should not have to change their traditional way of living. He was willing to go to war to protect these rights.

Childhood and Education

Jefferson Davis was born on June 3, 1808, in Christian County, Kentucky. The Davis family moved to Mississippi when Jefferson was still an infant. He was raised on a cotton **plantation** on which slaves were used. **Public education** was not as common in southern states as it was in northern states. Fortunately, Davis's family was able to send him to private schools. Davis entered the **United States Military Academy** at West Point when he was sixteen years old. He graduated in 1828, one year before Robert E. Lee.

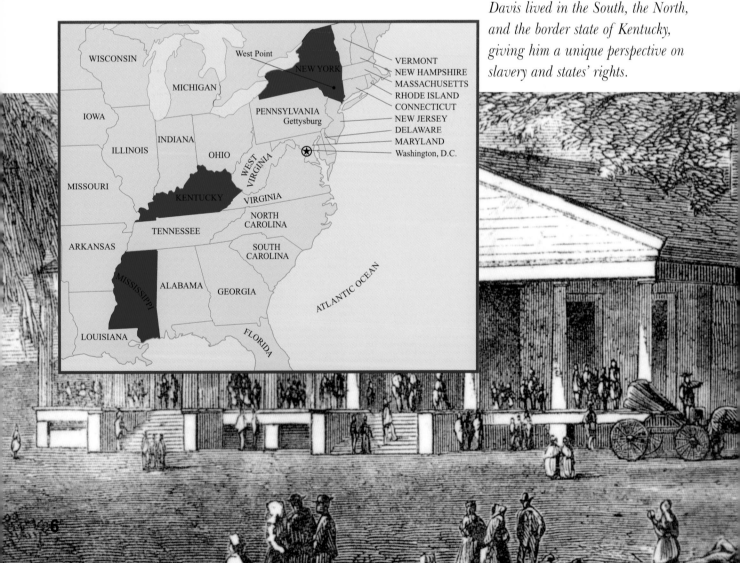

Davis lived in the South, the North, and the border state of Kentucky, giving him a unique perspective on slavery and states' rights.

Military Career

Davis then served in the United States Army for seven years. His first military assignment was as a soldier on the **frontier.** In 1835, Davis resigned, or gave up, his **commission** and returned to Mississippi to be a cotton planter. However, ten years later, he volunteered to fight in the Mexican War for the U.S. Army. He returned home to Mississippi a war hero. His military education at West Point followed by service in the U.S. Army helped him prepare for his leadership role during the Civil War.

Jefferson Davis lived in a mansion on his plantation in Mississippi.

This portrait of Jefferson Davis was taken while he was president of the Confederate States of America.

Political Career

Davis became interested in politics in the early 1840s. He won a seat in the **U.S. House of Representatives** in 1845. After returning from the Mexican War, Davis was picked to finish the **term** of a U.S. senator who had died. He later was elected to this position. He served in the **Senate** until 1850.

In 1853, Davis was appointed secretary of war for the U.S. government under President Franklin Pierce. Davis gained valuable experience during this term—experience that would help him guide the Confederacy. In 1857, he was again elected to the United States Senate for the state of Mississippi. In 1861, Mississippi **seceded** from the **Union,** and Davis resigned and returned home.

Davis served as the President of the Confederate States of America from February 1861 until the war ended in April 1865. He lived in Montgomery, Alabama, the site of the first Confederate capital. In May of 1861, he moved the capital city to Richmond, Virginia.

Davis, as president of the Confederacy, often had important papers brought to him in the field to be signed.

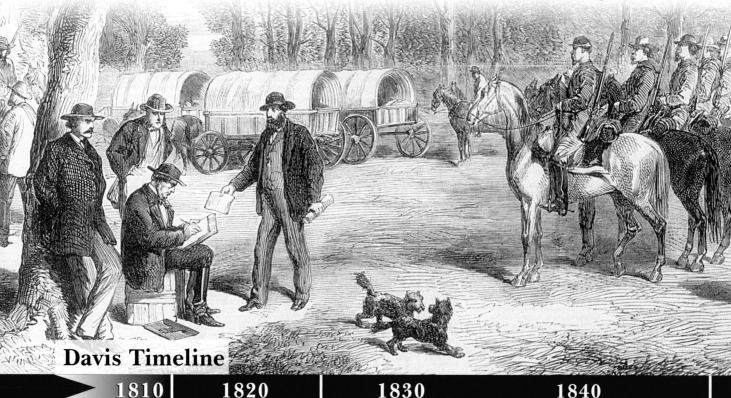

Davis Timeline

1810	1820	1830	1840
6/3/08 Born	1828 Graduates from West Point 1828 U.S. Army soldier assigned to the **frontier**		1845 Serves as a U.S. Representative for Mississippi 1846 Joins U.S. Army to fight in Mexican War 1847–1851 elected to U.S. Senate for Mississippi

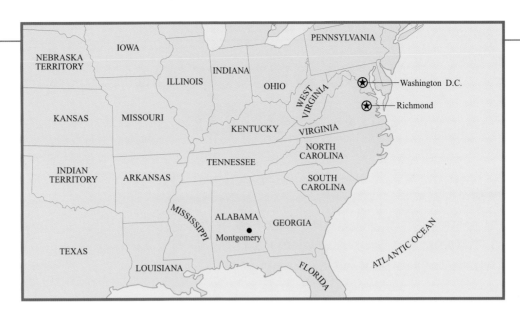

Richmond, Virginia, is located less than 100 miles (161 kilometers) from Washington, D.C. The capture of the capital of the Confederacy became a key objective for the Union Army.

War Years

Davis suffered through ill health during the war. He was criticized for his management of the war and often had problems with the southern congress. As the war dragged on, Davis was greatly saddened by the destruction of the South. As Union forces approached Richmond in the spring of 1865, Davis and his family fled the city. He was captured in Georgia soon after General Lee surrendered at Appomattox, ending the war. Davis spent two years in prison at a military base in Virginia called Fortress Monroe. In 1867, he was freed.

Final Years

Davis went home to Mississippi to farm the **plantation** he left behind. But the farm failed, and the family had to rely on a wealthy citizen for support. Davis later wrote a book about the Confederacy called *The Rise and Fall of the Confederate Government*. Davis died in Mississippi in 1889, at the age of 81. At the time of his death, he still believed that secession and slavery were best for the South.

This photo shows Jefferson Davis and three generations of his family in 1885.

1850	1860	1870	1880
1853–1857 Serves as U.S. Secretary of War	**1/9/61** Mississippi secedes from Union		**12/6/89** Dies
1857–1861 Again becomes senator for Mississippi	**1861** January, resigns from U.S. Senate		
	1861 Appointed President of Confederacy		
	1865 Captured and sent to prison		
	1867 Freed from prison, returns to Mississippi		

Economy of the South

Before the Civil War, crops grown on southern farms were in demand in factories in the North and in Europe. When the war began, however, the Union set up blockades to prevent goods from leaving the South. Southern cotton planters were left with no way to sell their cotton.

These same Union blockades also kept goods from other countries from entering the South. Northerners were not allowed to sell things to the South. The southern **economy** collapsed.

The Union blockaded all of the South's major seaports.

Money

As in the North, the Civil War caused major changes in the handling and distribution of money in the South. Before the war, people paid debts with gold and silver coins or traded goods or services. Once the war began, businesses needed a way to pay for buying and selling items to each other. Individual states, banks, and businesses decided to print their own designs of paper money for trading. And in 1861, the Confederate government also issued paper money to pay war bills. Few new coins were made. Once the war was over, the Confederacy was dissolved. Confederate paper money was not accepted by the United States Government and therefore, was worthless.

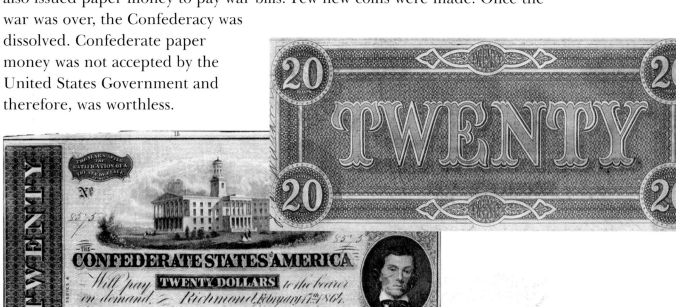

The Confederate twenty-dollar note included a photo of Confederate Vice President Alexander Stephens.

Rising Costs and Inflation

Inflation occurs when too many people want to buy a limited number of available products. The prices of these products rise, making it harder and harder for people to buy the things they need—especially people who have less money to spend.

Because the South's economy was based on the growing and selling of cotton, many southern farmers had large amounts of cotton to sell. However, few southern mills could turn this cotton into finished goods. The mills did not need all the cotton that farmers had to sell. Therefore, farmers had to sell their cotton cheaply, or the mills would buy it from another planter.

To make matters worse, there were not many southern factories, and most were needed to make war equipment. Products that farmers needed, such as farm equipment and seed, were scarce and therefore very expensive. And because farmers were not making much money, they could not afford these expensive items. These conditions created inflation, which caused many businesses to fail.

NOTICE.

RICHMOND, FREDERICKSBURG AND POTOMAC RAILROAD.

By a resolution of the Board of Public Works adopted on the 20th day of July, 1864, the tolls on freights over this Road were authorized to be ten times the rates of toll established by the Board of Directors on the 1st of May, 1861, which rates were by the Board of Directors of this Company adopted on the 27th of July, 1864, except as to tolls on wood, which were then established at eight times the rate fixed by the tariff of May 1, 1861.

☞To take effect August 1, 1864.

Rising costs reflected the poor health of the South's economy.

Slavery in the South

Slavery existed throughout the world long before the American Civil War began. In the United States, slavery was more widespread in the South than in the North. Most southern farms were small and did not use slaves. Cotton plantations kept slavery alive into the Civil War.

The slaves' main duty was to work in the fields. They also performed many other tasks that helped the daily lives of the plantation owner's family. Slaves did household chores, such as cooking and cleaning. They repaired buildings and took care of farm animals. Slaves were one way by which a large plantation could make money.

No Legal Rights

According to the U.S. Supreme Court ruling in the Dred Scott case, slaves were not citizens. They had no legal rights, and they could be bought and sold as personal property. Young, healthy, male slaves were worth the most money.

During the war, slaves continued to work on plantations. At times, they were taken from plantations to do **manual labor** for the war effort.

Life of a Slave

- Slaves could not vote.
- Slaves could not attend school.
- Slaves were often separated from their families.
- Slaves did not receive pay for working.
- Slaves could not leave the property without permission from their owners.

The primary duty of slaves on a cotton plantation was to work in the fields.

Emancipation

In September 1862, five days after the Battle of Antietam, President Lincoln issued a **preliminary** Emancipation Proclamation. This document stated that beginning on January 1, 1863, all slaves in Confederate states fighting against the Union would be set free if those states did not return to the Union. However, since Union troops could not enforce the law during the war, this proclamation had little effect until the war ended in April of 1865.

The Thirteenth Amendment to the U.S. Constitution

Not until December 16, 1865, did the U.S. Congress ratify, or pass, the Thirteenth **Amendment** to the **U.S. Constitution,** officially freeing all slaves.

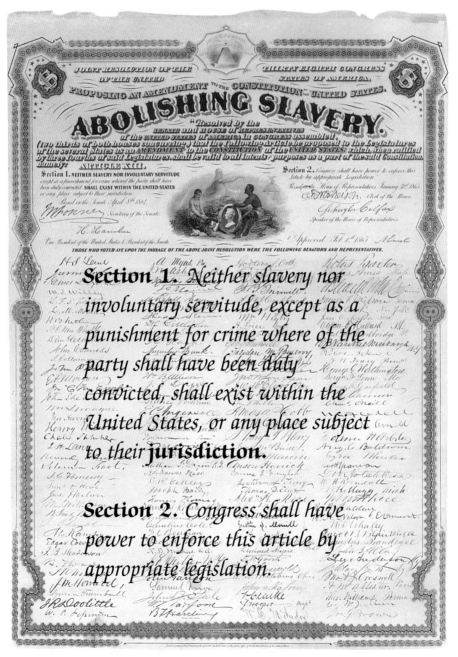

The 38th Congress voted to put an end to the practice of slavery throughout the nation.

Prior to the Thirteenth Amendment to the Constitution, slaves could be sold as property at public auction houses.

Life on a Southern Plantation

At the beginning of the Civil War, life on a large plantation continued as usual. Plantation owners grew one main crop to sell. Cotton was the most popular cash crop because it was in demand throughout the world at this time.

Tobacco, rice, and sugar were other major crops grown on plantations. Most plantation owners also grew a variety of crops for their own use. The families of large plantation owners did not do much heavy farm work—slaves did it for them. But as the Civil War continued, plantation life began to change.

On Southern plantations, a white overseer was responsible for watching the slaves as they worked in the fields.

Men

Many white male plantation owners joined the Confederate Army. Some owners paid substitutes to take their places in the army. According to the "Twenty Negro Law," a plantation owner did not have to join the army if he owned at least twenty slaves.

Plantations owners who were not in the army spent much of their time managing the business. Some of their responsibilities included arranging for crops to be sold, buying and selling slaves, and ordering equipment and supplies. Older sons or hired white men made sure the daily operations of the plantation ran smoothly. This gave owners time to follow other interests, such as local politics and recreational activities.

Male slaves primarily worked in the fields. They, along with women and children slaves, did the actual planting and harvesting of crops. Some male slaves were given other jobs that were necessary to keep the plantation running.

This photograph shows a reenactment of a Christmas celebration in a Confederate home during the Civil War, complete with the Confederate flag on the tree.

Women

The white women who lived on **plantations** organized the work inside the homes. But slaves did the actual house work. Plantation owner's wives and daughters kept busy doing needlework, arranging flowers, visiting with other women in the community, writing letters, or planning parties. As male family members left to be soldiers, many women had to do chores they previously were not expected to do, such as handling the business responsibilities of the plantation.

Female slaves did household chores, such as cooking, baking, and laundry. They helped care for the children in the plantation owners' families. Female slaves also worked outdoors in gardens and even in the large crop fields.

While women slaves worked on chores around the plantation house, the white women found time for leisure activities, such as playing croquet, like this family in Virginia is doing.

Female slaves often spent more time with the plantation owner's children than with their own.

Children

Children of plantation owners did little work. Younger plantation children spent most of their time studying, often with the help of **tutors.** However, when the war began, some tutors went to war, so the lessons stopped. Older male children often attended private schools and then went to college. During the war, many schools and colleges closed, as teachers and students volunteered or were **drafted** to be soldiers. For recreation, many boys enjoyed riding horses, hunting, and fishing. Girls often enjoyed music, drawing, and sewing.

Unlike white children living on a plantation, slave children had daily chores to do. These chores included pulling weeds and picking insects off of crops. Slave children were not permitted to attend school. They often were separated from their mothers, fathers, brothers, and sisters. Slaves were bought and sold as personal property by plantation owners.

Effects of War

Plantations faced greater hardships the longer the war lasted. **Union blockades** made it almost impossible for the South to export its cash crops. Also, most battles were fought on southern soil, destroying crops and land. Many plantation mansions crumbled.

The Potter House, shown here, was heavily damaged during the Civil War.

Living with the War

- Beginning in 1863, the Confederate government took a portion of each farmer's crops to feed its soldiers.

- Replacement parts, new machinery, and farming tools were difficult to purchase during the Civil War years. Factories were busy manufacturing products for the war.

- Soldiers from both armies took food and livestock from farms as they needed them.

- Slaves were often taken to work for the Confederate Army.

- Near the end of the war, the Union Army burned southern land as a way to destroy the South and stop the war.

Life on a Small Southern Farm

In 1861, most people in the South lived on small farms. These farmers usually did not own slaves. Life on a small southern farm became more difficult as the war progressed.

Ideal weather conditions, rich soil, and flat landscapes made it possible for southern farmers to grow many different types of crops and raise a variety of **livestock.** Unlike the owners of the large **plantations,** most small farmers raised crops mainly to feed their families. Many also grew a crop such as cotton to sell. Because there were no slaves, all family members worked to keep a small farm operating, including working in the fields.

The Civil War had as much of an impact on small southern farms as it did on the larger plantations.

Men

Men usually did the outdoor work, which included taking care of crops and livestock. Chores, such as milking, cleaning the barns, and feeding the animals were done daily. Throughout the year, land had to be cleared, soil prepared, seeds planted, and crops harvested. Most work was done without machines. Farmers turned the soil with a horse-drawn plow and planted seeds and harvested most crops by hand. After crops were planted, farmers had more time to cut firewood and repair fences and buildings. Farmers in a neighborhood would get together to build barns and harvest crops.

Women

Farmers' wives and daughters did most household chores. These chores included cooking, baking, washing dishes, doing laundry, cleaning house, and sewing. Women also did outdoor work, such as gardening. Women, children, and older family members did all the work when the men left the farm to fight in the war.

Many small farms did not have high-powered equipment.
The work had to be done by members of the family.

Children

Children who lived on small farms usually did daily chores. Even very young farm children were expected to do their share of work. Boys and girls would chop fire wood to use for cooking and heating. They would also help clean barns, feed animals, gather eggs, and milk cows.

Most schools closed during the war. Since most battles were fought on southern soil, school houses could be part of a battlefield. Men who were teachers often enlisted or were forced to become soldiers.

This family is doing chores on their small farm near Cedar Mountain, Virginia.

Effects of War

It was difficult for farming to continue as usual during the war. Most able men were in the army, and most battles were fought on southern soil.

Many fields and farmhouses were destroyed as battles raged across the South.

Living with the War

- Beginning in 1863, the Confederate government took a portion of each farmer's crops to feed its soldiers.

- Soldiers from both armies took food and livestock from farms as they needed it. Soldiers and equipment trampled fields and crops.

- Near the end of the war, land was burned as a way to destroy the South and stop the war.

Cities in the South

According to the U.S. Census Bureau, in 1860, more than 61,000 people lived in Richmond, Virginia, more than 70,000 people lived in Charleston, South Carolina, and more than 35,000 people lived in Montgomery, Alabama. Along with New Orleans, Louisiana, and Mobile, Alabama, these were some of the larger southern cities.

*The **docks** of New Orleans were a bustle of activity in 1862, with horse-drawn carriages and paddleboats waiting to **transport** cotton.*

The large southern cities were usually built around factories or geographic features, such as rivers or natural harbors. Many wealthy owners of factories built large mansions on tree-lined streets. Unlike large cities in the North, most city streets in the South were not paved. Four years of war had taken a toll on the Confederate States of America. By the end of the war in 1865, fighting had destroyed many of the most important southern cities.

Ideas and Inventions

The population of the South was less than half the population of the North. To overcome this huge disadvantage in manpower, the South needed to try new ideas and inventions.

Southern technology helped to **prolong** the war for the South. Unfortunately, most of these ideas had some type of **flaw** that kept them from being effective.

Confederate railways in the South brought much-needed supplies to the soldiers.

The Confederate Army

The Confederate Army was first to **transport** troops on railroad cars into battle. They also tried to use hot air balloons to observe enemy troops. Southern inventors developed a type of grenade and machine gun that had only a small amount of success.

The Southern Navy

At the start of the Civil War, the newly formed Confederate Navy did not have ships that were ready for battle, except for those seized when the states **seceded** from the **Union.**

Confederate Firsts:

- The Confederacy was the first to put an ironclad ship into battle. The CSS *Virginia (Merrimac)* had a wooden bottom with thick steel plates covering the top to two feet below the water level. It had a ram and guns.

- Small torpedo boats called "Davids" were designed to ram into an enemy boat, and then set off explosives.

- H.L. Hunley invented a submarine. It sank the USS *Housatonic*, but also sank itself.

Confederate torpedo gunboats, like this "David" shown here in Charleston, South Carolina, were designed to sink Union ships.

Defeat

Crops were ruined, land was destroyed, major cities and small towns were demolished, tens of thousands of soldiers were dead, and the southern economy was shattered. The Confederacy was forced to surrender.

Under new **Federal** laws, slaves were free and given U.S. citizenship, but most had no money and no land. Survival for them would be difficult. As planters tried to rebuild their **plantations,** many former slaves stayed to work as hired hands or **sharecroppers.**

The U.S. Congress placed **Union** troops in the southern states to make sure citizens obeyed the new laws. Everyone knew it would take southerners a long time to adjust to this different way of life. The **traditional** southern way of life could not exist as it had before the Civil War.

Charleston, South Carolina, was one of man southern cities left in ruins after the Civil W

A Future of Rebuilding

Southern states needed to be officially readmitted as states of the Union. Citizens had to promise to obey all new laws, including allowing freed slave men the right to vote. It took four years to readmit the eleven southern states that had **seceded** at the beginning of the war.

As each state returned to the Union, all of the slaves became free citizens.

State	Date Rejoined the Union
Tennessee	July 24, 1866
Arkansas	June 22, 1868
Florida	June 25, 1868
North Carolina	July 4, 1868
Louisiana	July 9, 1868
South Carolina	July 9, 1868
Alabama	July 13, 1868
Virginia	January 26, 1870
Mississippi	February 23, 1870
Texas	March 30, 1870
Georgia	July 15, 1870

Glossary

amendment   part of the U.S. Constitution that was changed or added

blockade   to close off or stop people or supplies from reaching a place

commission   appointment by the president of a country to serve as an officer in the military

dock   platform near a pier for loading and unloading ships

drafted   to be required to enter military service

economy   management of money and the making and selling of goods

federal   of or relating to a nation formed by the Union of several states; the Union in the Civil War

flaw   defect

frontier   edge of the settled part of a country

manual labor   work done by hand without the help of a machine

plantation   large farm on which crops are tended by laborers who also live there

preliminary   coming before the main event or part; introductory

prolong   last longer

public education   free schooling paid for by taxes and managed by a local government

secede   to leave the Union

Senate   part of the U.S. Congress that helps to write federal laws

sharecropper   farmer who used crops as payment to rent land

term   specific amount of time

territory   land in the United States that was not a state

traditional   handed down from generation to generation

transport   to carry from one location to another

tutor   person who teaches another, usually outside a school setting

Union   another name for the United States of America; during the Civil War it referred to the states that remained loyal to the United States government

United States Military Academy   college that teaches men and women to be officers in the U.S. Army

U.S. Census Bureau   department of the U.S. government that is in charge of counting how many people live in the United States

U.S. Constitution   document that establishes the form of government of the United States and defines the rights and liberties of the American people

U.S. House of Representatives   part of the U.S. Congress that helps to write federal laws

Historical Fiction to Read

Beatty, Patricia. *Turn Homeward, Hannalee*. New York: William Morrow & Co., 1984.
Textile workers in Georgia, including a twelve-year-old girl, are taken north to work in a Union mill. The twelve year old is determined to return to Georgia and her family.

McKissack, Patricia. *A Picture of Freedom: The Diary of Clotee, a Slave Girl, Belmont Plantation, Virginia, 1859*. New York: Scholastic, Inc., 1997.
Thirteen-year-old Clotee keeps a secret diary of her experiences as a slave on a Virginia Plantation in 1859.

Turner, Ann. *Nettie's Trip South*. New York: Scholastic, 1987.
A young girl from Albany, New York, visits the South and witnesses slavery for the first time.

Civil War Places to Visit

Arlington House/The Robert E. Lee Memorial
George Washington Memorial Parkway
Turkey Run Park, McLean, Virginia 22101
Telephone: (703) 557-0613
Arlington House provides an intimate look at Robert E. Lee's life before and after the Civil War. Here, in 1861, General Lee wrote the letter resigning his commission from the U.S. Army to fight for his native Virginia. The house is restored with many furnishings that were originally owned by Lee's family, showing how a wealthy southern family lived.

Kent Plantation House
3601 Bayou Rapides Road
Alexandria, Louisiana 71303
Telephone: (318) 487-5998
With its gardens and slave cabins, plantation kitchen and barn,
the site depicts the history of central Louisiana from 1795 through 1855.

Meadow Farm Museum
Henrico Division of Recreation and Parks
P.O. Box 27032
Richmond, Virginia 23273
Telephone: (804) 501-5520
Meadow Farm is an 1860 living history farm focusing on middle-class rural life just before the upheaval of the Civil War. Costumed interpreters provide insights into the lives of Dr. John Mosby Sheppard, the owner of Meadow Farm, and his family.

The Museum of the Confederacy
1201 East Clay Street
Richmond, Virginia 23219
Telephone: (804) 649-1861
This museum maintains the world's largest collection of military, political, and home front artifacts and art from the period of the Confederacy, 1861–1865. The museum includes the restored historic White House of the Confederacy.

Index